101 Girls Basketball Motivational Quotes

Patosha Jeffery

Copyright © 2014 Patosha Jeffery

All rights reserved.

ISBN: 1500419370
ISBN-13: 978-1500419370

DEDICATION

To the men and women dedicated to working with young ladies in the game of basketball.

Before every practice at the University of Memphis, my coach would gather the team at the circle on the court for announcements and the quote of the day. I got a kick out of the quotes and loved giving my interpretations of their meanings. When I became a coach, it became a practice of mine to huddle my team up for announcements and give a quote of the day. Motivational quotes provide inspiration, hope and even a sense of direction. They're great for practices, games and off the court encouragement. You can come up with different ways to use motivational quotes. Type a quote(s) up and provide for your team in your team notebook. Print them up on small strips of paper to provide before game day or the morning of game day. Have a quote painted on the wall of the team locker room. The uses of motivational quotes are endless.

1. "You become what you think about."
   — *Earl Nightingale*

2. "People with goals succeed because they know where they are going... It's as simple as that."
   — *Earl Nightingale*

3. "You, too, can determine what you want. You can decide on your major objectives, targets, aims, and destination."
   — *W. Clement Stone*

4. "The indispensable first step to getting the things you want out of life is this: decide what you want."
   — *Ben Stein*

5. "The most important thing about goals is having one."
   — *Geoffry F. Abert*

6. "This one step, choosing a goal and sticking to it, changes everything."
   — *Scott Reed*

7. "There is one quality that one must possess to win, and that is definiteness of purpose, the knowledge of

what one wants, and a burning desire to possess it."
— *Napoleon Hill*

8. "Visualize this thing you want. See it, feel it, believe in it. Make your mental blueprint and begin. "
— *Robert Collier*

9. "Patience and perseverance have a magical effect before which difficulties disappear and obstacles vanish."
— *John Quincy Adams*

10. "I do not think there is any other quality so essential to success of any kind as the quality of perseverance. It overcomes almost everything, even nature."
— *John D. Rockefeller*

11. "The only thing that stands between a man and what he wants from life is often merely the will to try it and the faith to believe that it is possible."
— *Richard M. DeVos*

12. "All who have accomplished great things have had a great aim, have fixed their gaze on a goal which was high, one which sometimes seemed impossible."
— *Orison Swett Marden*

13. "Aim for success not perfection... Remember that fear always lurks behind perfectionism. Confronting your fears and allowing yourself the right to be human can, paradoxically, make you a far happier and more productive person."
    — *Dr. David Burns*

14. "Time is our most valuable asset, yet we tend to waste it, kill it, and spend it rather than invest it."
    — *Jim Rohn*

15. "You may have a fresh start any moment you choose, for this thing that we call "failure" is not the falling down, but the staying down."
    — *Mary Pickford*

16. "Success is never final and failure never fatal. It is courage that counts."
    — *George F. Tilton*

17. "Fight one more round. When your arms are so tired that you can hardly lift your hands to come on guard, fight one more round. When your nose is bleeding and your eyes are black and you are so tired that you wish your opponent would crack you one on the jaw and put you to sleep, fight one more round – remembering that the man who always fights one

more round is never whipped."
— *James Corbett*

18. "Big goals get big results. No goals get no results or somebody else's results."
— *Mark Victor Hansen*

19. "Do a little more each day than you think you can."
— *Lowell Thomas*

20. "Satisfaction lies in the effort, not in the attainment. Full effort is full victory."
— *Mohandas Gandhi*

21. "When you believe you can-you can!"
— *Maxwell Maltz*

22. "When you get right down to the root of the meaning of the word 'succeed,' you find that it simply means to follow through."
— *F. W. Nichol*

23. "I am an irresistible magnet, with the power to attract unto myself everything that I divinely desire, according to the thoughts, feelings and mental pictures I constantly entertain and radiate. I am the center of my universe! I have the power to create

whatever I wish. I attract whatever I radiate. I attract whatever I mentally choose and accept. I begin choosing and mentally accepting the highest and best in life. I now choose and accept health, success and happiness. I now choose lavish abundance for myself and for all mankind. This is a rich, friendly universe and I dare to accept its riches, its hospitality, and to enjoy them now!"
— *Catherine Ponde*

24. "The obstacles that others put in our path can be pushed aside in any number of ways. The obstacles that you put in your own way can be removed only by the same hands."
— *Sophia Bedford-Pierce*

25. "If you decide to go for it, do it with spirit: Sometimes success is due less to ability than to zeal."
— *Charles Buxton*

26. "Our greatest glory consists not in never falling... but in rising every time we fall."
— *Ralph Waldo Emerson*

27. "Movement without direction will create a hole in the ground."
— *Sophia Bedford-Pierce*

28. "Everything's in the mind. That's where it all starts. Knowing what you want is the first step toward getting it."
— *Mae West*

29. "When your desires are strong enough you will appear to possess superhuman powers to achieve."
— *Napoleon Hill*

30. "Everything you want in life has a price connected to it. There's a price to pay if you want to make things better, a price to pay just for leaving things as they are, a price for everything."
— *Harry Browne*

31. "Never leave that till tomorrow which you can do today."
— *Benjamin Franklin*

32. "The successful person has the habit of doing the things failures don't like to do. They don't like doing them either necessarily. But their disliking is

subordinated to the strength of their purpose."
— *E.M. Gray*

33. "Keep your eyes on the stars and your feet on the ground."
— *Theodore Roosevelt*

34. "Climb high; climb far. Your goal is the sky; your aim is the star."
— *Inscription at Williams College*

35. "It is impossible to win the race unless you venture to run, impossible to win the victory unless you dare to battle."
— *Richard M. DeVos*

36. "Our thoughts and imaginations are the only real limits to our possibilities."
— *Ralph Waldo Trine*

37. "The only way to discover the limits of the possible is to go beyond them into the impossible."
— *Arthur C. Clarke*

38. "Reduce your plan to writing... The moment you complete this, you will have definitely given concrete

form to the intangible desire."
— *Napoleon Hill*

39. "It's not whether you get knocked down, it's whether you get up."
— *Vince Lombardi*

40. "One cannot get through life without pain... What we can do is choose how to use the pain life presents to us."
— *Bernie Siegel*

41. "The wise man bridges the gap by laying out the path by means of which he can get from where he is to where he wants to go."
— *John Morgan and Ewing Webb*

42. "Success is never final and failure never fatal. It's courage that counts. "
— *George F. Tiltonood*

43. "Nothing happens unless first a dream."
— *Carl Sandburg*

44. "What the mind can conceive and believe, it can achieve."
— *Napoleon Hill*

45. "Imagination is more important than knowledge."
— *Albert Einstein*

46. "Vision is the art of seeing the invisible."
— *Jonathan Swift*

47. "If you don't set goals for yourself, you are doomed to work to achieve the goals of someone else."
— *Brian Tracy*

48. "You miss a 100 percent of the shots you don't take."
— *Wayne Gretzky*

49. "Don't bother just to be better than your contemporaries or predecessors. Try to be better than yourself."
— *William Faulkner*

50. "Only those who risk going too far can possibly know how far one can go."
— *T.S. Elliot*

51. "Nothing is particularly hard if you divide it into small jobs."
— *Henry Ford*

52. "There are no secrets to success. It is the result of preparation, hard work, and learning from failure."
— *Colin Powell*

53. "Winners are those people who make a habit of doing the things losers are uncomfortable doing."
— *Ed Foreman*

54. "A good plan today is better than a great plan tomorrow."
— *General George S. Patton*

55. "Do not wait; the time will never be 'just right'. Start where you stand, and work with whatever tools you may have at your command, and better tools will be found as you go along."
— *Napoleon Hill*

56. "It's not what you are that holds you back, it's what you think you are not."
— *Denis Waitley*

57. "We should not let our fears hold us back from pursuing our hopes."
— *John F. Kennedy*

58. "You must begin to think of yourself as becoming the person you want to be."
— *David Viscott*

59. "We tend to get what we expect."
— *Norman Vincent Peale*

60. "Don't let what you cannot do interfere with what you can do."
— *John Wooden*

61. "The one without dreams is the one without wings."
— *Muhammad Ali*

62. "Most misfortunes are the results of misused time."
— *Napoleon Hill*

63. "You do not merely want to be considered just the best of the best. You want to be considered the only one who does what you do."
— *Jerry Garcia*

64. "If you want the rainbow, you've got to put up with the rain."
— *Jimmy Durante*

65. "Every winner has scars."
— *Herbert N. Casson*

66. "Goals are new, forward-moving objectives. They magnetize you towards them."
— *Mark Victor Hansen*

67. "People of mediocre ability sometimes achieve outstanding success because they don't know when to quit. Most people succeed because they are determined to. "
— *George E. Allen*

68. "You may get skinned knees and elbows, but it's worth it if you score a spectacular goal."
— *Mia Hamm*

69. "Opportunity is missed by most people because it is dressed in overalls and looks like work."
— *Thomas A. Edison*

70. "The ability to discipline yourself to delay gratification in the short term in order to enjoy greater rewards in the long term is the indispensable prerequisite for success."
— *Brian Tracy*

71. "If you're never scared or embarrassed or hurt, it means you never take any chances."
— *Julia Sorel*

72. "Success is a journey, not a destination."
— *Ben Sweetland*

73. "The journey is the reward."
— *Taoist Proverb*

74. "There is always room at the top."
— *Daniel Webster*

75. "Success is never final."
— *Winston Churchill*

76. "Things turn out best for the people who make the best of the way things turn out."
— *John Wooden*

77. "The men who try to do something and fail are infinitely better than those who try to do nothing and succeed."
— *Lloyd Jones*

78. "He that walketh with wise men shall be wise..."
— *Bible, Proverbs 13:20*

79. "Failure is, in a sense, the highway to success..."
— *John Keats*

80. "Mistakes are merely steps up the ladder..."
— *Paul J. Meyer*

81. "Some defeats are only installments to victory."
— *Jacob A. Riis*

82. "The man who makes no mistakes does not usually make anything."
— *William Connor Magee*

83. "I am not discouraged, because every wrong attempt discarded is another step forward."
— *Thomas A. Edison*

84. "To win...you've got to stay in the game..."
— *Claude M. Bristol*

85. "You can do what you think you can do and you cannot do what you think you cannot do."
— *Ben Stein*

86. "Your chances of success in any undertaking can always be measured by your belief in yourself."
— *Robert Collier*

87. "The mind is the limit. As long as the mind can envision the fact that you can do something, you can do it – as long as you really believe a 100 percent."
— *Arnold Schwarzenegger*

88. "The hand cannot reach higher than does the heart."
— *Orison Swett Marden*

89. "The only limits are, as always, those of vision."
— *James Broughton*

90. "Our aspirations are our possibilities"
— *Robert Browning*

91. "We've got to have a dream if we are going to make a dream come true."
— *Denis Waitley*

92. "Knowing that you have complete control of your thinking you will recognize the power..."
— *Mikhail Strabo*

93. "The greatest discovery of my generation is that human beings can alter their lives by altering their

attitudes of mind."
— *William James*

94. "You are where you are today because you've chosen to be there."
— *Harry Browne*

95. "How things look on the outside of us depends on how things are on the inside of us."
— *Parks Cousins*

96. "What's going on in the inside shows on the outside."
— *Earl Nightingale*

97. "You cannot have success without the failures."
— *H. G. Hasler*

98. "Every failure brings with it the seed of an equivalent success."
— *Napoleon Hill*

99. "Any experience can be transformed into something of value."
— *Vash Young*

100. "View every problem as an opportunity..."
— *Joseph Sugarman*

101. "Singleness of purpose is one of the chief essentials for success in life, no matter what may be one's aim."
— *John D. Rockefeller*

ABOUT THE AUTHOR

Patosha Jeffery is the founder of Patosha Jeffery Basketball, a girls basketball performance development company dedicated to helping players understand basketball in order to play at a high level and possibly at the collegiate level. She is also the founder of MemphisGirlsBasketball.com and the Memphis Girls Basketball Fall Fest, which includes the Fall Exposure League and Pre-Season Show Off Camp.

Patosha was a talented player at the junior high and high school levels. She accepted a college athletic scholarship at the University of Memphis. However, she had some periods of struggle on the court while in high school and on the collegiate level. Those struggles inspired her to mentor players through their hardships and struggles in basketball and to help them obtain a college athletic scholarship. Since then, she has mentored numerous players and helped dozens get scholarships and play college basketball at schools like Arkansas State, Auburn, Colorado, Florida, Georgia Tech, Louisville, Memphis, Southern Mississippi, and Ole Miss.

Learn more about Patosha, her events and products at patoshajeffery.com.

Made in the USA
Lexington, KY
16 December 2017